Summary of The Total Money Makeover & Summary of The Untethered Soul

By: Dave Ramsey

Proudly Brought to you by:

Text Copyright © Readtrepreneur

All rights reserved. No part of this guide may be reproduced in any form without permission in writing from the publisher except in the case of brief quotations embodied in critical articles or reviews.

Legal & Disclaimer

The information contained in this book is not designed to replace or take the place of any form of medicine or professional medical advice. The information in this book has been provided for educational and entertainment purposes only.

The information contained in this book has been compiled from sources deemed reliable, and it is accurate to the best of the Author's knowledge; however, the Author cannot guarantee its accuracy and validity and cannot be held liable for any errors or omissions. Changes are periodically made to this book. You must consult your doctor or get professional medical advice before using any of the suggested remedies, techniques, or information in this book. Images used in this book are not the same as of those of the actual book. This is a totally separate and different entity from that of the original book titled: "The Total Money Makeover"

Upon using the information contained in this book, you agree to hold harmless the Author from and against any damages, costs, and expenses, including any legal fees potentially resulting from the application of any of the information provided by this guide. This disclaimer applies to any damages or injury caused by the use and application, whether directly or indirectly, of any advice or information presented, whether for breach of contract, tort, negligence, personal injury, criminal intent, or under any other cause of action.

You agree to accept all risks of using the information presented inside this book. You need to consult a professional medical practitioner in order to ensure you are both able and healthy enough to participate in this program.

Table of Contents

The Book at a Glance 7

Introduction 10

What This Book Is Not 12

Flying Turkeys and Skinny Dipping 16

Chapter 1: The Total Money Makeover Challenge 20

Chapter 2: Denial: I'm Not *That* Out of Shape 23

Chapter 3: Debt Myths: Debt Is (Not) a Tool 26

Chapter 4: Money Myths: The (Non)Secrets of the Rich 33

Chapter 5: Two More Hurdles: Ignorance and Keeping Up with the Joneses 38

Chapter 6: Save $1,000 Fast: Walk Before You Run
.... 41

Chapter 7: The Debt Snowball: Lose Weight Fast, Really 45

Chapter 8: Finish the Emergency Fund: Kick Murphy Out 49

Chapter 9: Maximize Retirement Investing: Be Financially Healthy for Life 52

Chapter 10: College Funding: Make Sure the Kids Are Fit Too 56

Chapter 11: Pay Off the Home Mortgage: Be Ultrafit 60

Chapter 12: Build Wealth Like Crazy: Arnold Schwarzedollar, Mr. Universe of Money 63

Chapter 13: Live Like No One Else 66

Meet The Winners of The Total Money Makeover Challenge 68

Conclusion 70

About the Author 73

FREE BONUSES 74

The Book at a Glance

The Total Money Makeover offers a proven plan to achieve financial fitness. The goal is to change a person's behavior towards money so he can experience freedom from debt and live his life to the fullest.

Chapter 1 describes what is considered normal for American families when it comes to money issues. It also explains the Makeover challenge, the motto of your Makeover, and the guaranteed result if you complete the challenge.

Chapter 2 explains why so many people are stuck with their unhealthy money-spending habits and not doing anything about it.Most people see debt as a normal part of life.

Chapter 3 dispels all the myths that proliferate regarding debt. There are also a lot of myths about money out there which usually involve lies about security and shortcut.

Chapter 4 exposes the truth about money myths.

Chapter 5 talks about two more hurdles that keep people from building wealth – ignorance and keeping up with the Joneses.

Chapter 6 is about the first step of your Total Money Makeover. It talks about the importance of having a written monthly budget and the emergency fund. It will teach you how to come up with the $1,000 quick.

Chapter 7 explains the second step – the Debt Snowball or how you can pay off your debt in a systematic way. It also tells you how to prioritize them and what to do with your other debts.

Chapter 8 is the third step, in which you must complete your emergency fund. It will teach you how much savings you must have and where you should put all that money.

Chapter 9 describes the fourth step – saving for your retirement. It will show you how to compute how much you should save each month so you could have a decent life in your golden age.

Chapter 10 shows you what your options are in terms of funding your kids' college education. Making sure your kids are also financially fit is the fifth step.

Chapter 11 is the sixth step of your Makeover – paying off your home mortgage. It also dispels some myths about mortgage.

Chapter 12 is the last step – when you're already debt free

and building wealth. It will teach you the best things you could do with your wealth.

Finally, Chapter 13 serves as a reminder about the point of your Makeover to keep you from the biggest problem regarding wealth.

Introduction

Personal finance is more of how you behave than what you know. Most people know what to do with money, but only a few have any idea how to do it. So financial people simply showing you the numbers may not be of any help. Wealth building is simple but only if you learn to behave.

This Total Money Makeover plan has been proven to be effective. Not because it will reveal to you the secrets of the rich but because it will encourage you to change your life. And doing so will not only free you from debt but also result to better relationships.

Hope is an immense force. And this book has given hope to so many families to take action and overcome their financial struggles and uncertainties. This book has helped them win their financial battles.

The step-by-step process in this book is simple yet encouraging. Don't be surprised if you find that the principles here are not very unique. They are your grandmothers'. They're common sense, which, unfortunately, isn't common these days. This book will help you recognize and identify some everyday common sense and simple truths which have helped millions to change their lives and have a Total Money Makeover.

What This Book Is Not

For you to be able to decide if this book is worth-spending your hard-earned money on, it is proper to let you know what this book is not.

This Book Is Not Sophisticated or Complicated

This is not painstakingly detailed guide to investing. Nor is it an academic chirping that uses words to validate the author's ego.

We are made to believe that simple ideas are for the little minds. This is an incorrect and arrogant view. Many millionaires keep their financial thinking straightforward. In fact, some of the most life-changing truths you will learn are quite simple.

This Book is Not Something That Has Never Been Said

There's very little in this book that is original because this is mainly a compilation of long-standing information converted into a process that is attainable and has motivated millions to act on it.

This Book Is Not Going to Mislead You on Investment Returns

Many in this country today are ignorant when it comes to the returns of investing properly. They believe that making a 12% rate of return in a long-term investment is impossible. And that rate being available is a lie or a misleading statement.

The long-term investments recommended in this book are stock-type mutual funds, and through them, you should be able to make 12% on your money. Historical averages of the Standard & Poor's 500 index support that statement. It has averaged 11.67% per year since 1930s. With 500 of the biggest companies in principal industries of the US economy the S&P 500 index is considered by most experts as the best gauge of stock market returns. Practically every stock fund will present to you its returns in comparison to this index.

Any reasonable broker can direct you to funds averaging over 12% for a long period of time. So don't believe those who tell you that you can't expect a 12% rate when you're investing for at least 10 years.

This Book Is Not Written by Someone with No Academic Credentials

Although the author of this book considers academic and

financial credentials insignificant, he actually has a degree in finance and has been licensed in real estate, investments, and insurance. But he believes that what makes him suitable to teach about money is his many failures. He knows what it's like to be afraid, to have his marriage tested because of financial stress, and to have his hopes crushed by his own unwise decisions. Most of all, his book has freed hundreds of thousands of people across the country.

This Book Is Not Wrong

The principles discussed in this book have helped change the lives of many people. This book works and millions have already benefited from it.

This Book Is Not the Same as the Author's Other Books

Nearly two million copies of Financial Peace have already been sold. While many may think that this book says the same thing, there is actually more to it. Financial Peace is about money management. It tells its reader what to do with their money. But this book focuses on how to do what you want to do.

This Book Is Not Getting Any Complaints or Criticism...

...from those who apply what this book teaches. People who follow this plan are able to discover a new life. They are able to achieve financial freedom and their lives have forever been changed. If you want to go through the same transformation, start your Total Money Makeover today.

Flying Turkeys and Skinny Dipping

Most likely, you are familiar with the story of the three little pigs who built their own houses. One used straw, the other twigs, and the third built a house using bricks. The two short-term thinkers made fun of the bricklaying pig for spending too much time and effort to do it properly. But when the big bad wolf came huffing and puffing, the two lazy pigs found not only their houses blown apart but also their lives.

Economic Storms, Real Ones

In 2008, America was hit by a huge economic storm. The only companies that survived were those that were built well. Most of the businesses that deserted their solid foundations by putting their money in high-risk investments and taking huge debts are now history or acquired by someone else.

What happened?

Wanting to buy homes, broke people loaned money from greedy bankers at awful terms and high interest rates. Banks and investment bankers started buying lots of these loans in order to profit more and keep their stock prices high. This practice has become common in the investment community.

Using high-level financial instruments, formerly legitimate banks and investment bankers basically transformed into loan sharks. Unsurprisingly, the people who were in grave financial problems couldn't afford their mortgage payments. And there were a lot of them. So, the number of foreclosures increased rapidly. In markets where real estate prices were high, the foreclosures resulted to decreasing home prices.

With prices so low, responsible home-owners began facing trouble too. Stock prices on Wall Street started dropping. Through the news media, Americans watched hysteria every day. With the value of their homes and 401(k) plummeting, they decided to spend less.

The economy slowed and businesses were hurt. Lots of cash-poor companies and those that were deep in debt began to die. Manufacturers began laying off people and unemployment grew. This resulted to much lower real estate and stock prices.

Flying Turkeys

People learned their lessons from this event, either on a personal or national level. And the economy is continuously recovering. This event has permanently altered the way many people handled money.

The first lesson is that your financial principles must work in both the good and bad times. If not, they don't work. With a good economy, you can do stupid things with money. People say that even turkeys can fly in a tornado. People buy things they couldn't even afford. But when bad times came, their houses fell just like what happened to the two little pigs.

In the book *How the Mighty Fall*, James Collins talks about the five stages of decline of a failed business. The first stage is marked by arrogance that results to taking unreasonable risks. This arrogance initiates carelessness and denial of risk. People assume that the rules of risk don't apply to them. And so they build a house that can't even stand a light breeze.

Skinny-Dipping

You will know who was skinny-dipping once the tide goes out. If the map you have is terrible, you may miss the party. And the level of success you will achieve will depend on the principles you build your life on.

Overspending is overspending even if it doesn't feel like it. Investing in the stock market or real estate using borrowed money will cause you to go bankrupt the moment the market turns. Buying into scams that offer you a quick way to get rich will surely bring you pain. And hiring a debt-settlement company to resolve your

financial issues almost always fails.

Chapter 1: The Total Money Makeover Challenge

Many people feel like they are lost, out of control, and with no sense of power. They are troubled with financial issues; scared of monthly bills and terrified of thoughts about the future.

The "Normal" American Family

With very little savings, excessive debt, and no sense of control over their lives – that's the typical and normal American family. People work so hard but they are forever to be enslaved by bankers, the government, and their family's needs.

If you've felt you've had enough of feeling sick and tired of always worrying about your bills and working every single day just so you could pay your debts, and if you've realized that your nonplan isn't working, you're going to love this book.

At 26, Dave held a $4 million real estate. But his house was built of cards. When bad times came, he and his family lost everything. They were sued, foreclosed on, and went bankrupt. Scared and crushed, they still held on to each other decided that they needed a change.

After losing everything, Dave went to figure out how money truly works. He wanted to learn how to get control and handle it well. His quest led him to his mirror. He realized that the root of all his money problems is the man he sees in that mirror. And the only way to win at money is managing the character of that person.

The big challenge for you is to take on that per The Big Challenge: Find a Mirror

son you see in your mirror. If you think you're ready to take that challenge, you're set to win. There is a simple way to handle money. And yes, building wealth is no rocket science. But don't expect the process to be easy. Because if it was, every single one of us would be rich.

The Total Money Makeover challenge starts with you. You're the problem and the answer is also you. The plan is for you to pay all the prices that come with winning. And this plan works because it's simple. Some people pay the same price but still lose and that is because they didn't have what you have – a guaranteed plan for financial fitness.

The Total Money Makeover Motto

Live like no one else can today so that in the future, you can live like no one else. In your makeover, you will learn how to say "no." The willingness to postpone gratification for a better result is a sign of maturity. But some are too immature to pass up on pleasure. The sacrifices you will make will guarantee you a life that most people won't be able to live. The motto of your makeover is a reminder that you will win and what you will reap is worth the cost.

A Promise to You

You will be free from debt. You will save money and build your wealth. You will find yourself giving like you've never done before. That is a promise to you if you stick to the rules of this system of discipline and sacrifice. But keep in mind that this system will only work if you do your part.

Chapter 2: Denial: I'm Not *That* Out of Shape

For a person to get in shape, they must realize that there is a problem and they need to change thheir ways. Aside from that, they must also recognize any impediment that is keeping them from getting fit. The same applies for your Total Money Makeover.

Once you realize that you have a problem and you identify what it is, you already solved 90% of your problem. The biggest obstacle in resetting your money-spending habit is denial. The sad thing is that in this country, many people are okay with being financially mediocre. Being average is the standard to most.

The Wall Street Journal reported that 70% of American live paycheck to paycheck. Sara honestly thought that she was part of the 30% who were better off, but what she didn't realize is that she was in denial.

Sara and John were married with two kids. Their combined income was $75,000 per year. Their student and car loans, and $5,000 on credit card were considered normal. Thinking that their life was going well, they had a new home constructed. They moved in to their new home in May. Four months later, the company Sara was working for started downsizing and her job was the first to be eliminated. With $45,000 out of their annual income, they were suddenly facing repossession of their cars and foreclosure on the new house.

The couple had been listeners of *The Dave Ramsey Show* but they never thought they would ever need the Makeover. Only after Sara lost her job did they see financially fat people when they looked in the mirror; with huge house and car payments, student loans, bloated credit cards and virtually no savings.

It's hard to be in denial when you are physically fat. But when you're financially fat, you can fake it and with your family and friends taking part in your fantasy, you'll keep on believing that you're doing just fine. Sadly, most people have to have life smack them so hard before they realize that they need a makeover. And if something like that doesn't happen to you, you're in danger of suffering from financial mediocrity or a major crisis.

The Pain of Change

Most people are afraid of change because it's a painful process. Only when the pain of where they are tops the pain associated with change do they seek out change. The story of

Sara and the others are supposed to make you feel reluctant to remain where you are. If you're enjoying your current situation, keep it up. But don't forget the reason why you have this book. Do you have uneasy feeling buried deep down which should be addressed before it's too late? Do you want something more in your life? The plan in this book works and you'll be able to escape the pull of staying in the same situation.

*

The layoff finally ended Sara's denial. After a year of hardships, she was able to find a new job. Being under the Makeover, Sara and John planned every paycheck. They were in the process of losing weight financially.

Two years into the system, their only debt was for their house. For emergencies, they had $12,000 in the bank. They weren't in denial anymore although it had caused them their comfortable way of life. They stopped impressing other people with what they did with their money. While Sara hopes that none of them would ever lose another job all of a sudden, they were ready if in case it happened. The family isn't living a lie anymore.

Chapter 3: Debt Myths: Debt Is (Not) a Tool

It is in the nature of human to want something and want it at once. And this nature is an indication of immaturity. You may have witnessed a toddler screaming at the top of his lungs, demanding something that he desperately wants.

Maturity is postponing desire for even greater rewards. But our culture teaches us that we should live for the now. And for most, going into debt is the solution to getting what they want but cannot afford.

Joining in the Lie

If you tell the same lie long enough, that lie can soon be recognized as a fact. Repetition, longevity, and volume will transform a lie into an acceptable means of doing things. And this ridiculous thing has been happening all throughout history. Propaganda, specifically, had a big role in letting these things happen.

In our culture today, propaganda is used by people who want us to think like they do. Consider a car advertisement. Using attractive people to sell cars, ads make you believe that driving that certain car will make you look cool and sharp. You're aware it's not rational but you still buy that car and justify your purchase with something intellectual like gas mileage.

Don't Let the Monkeys Pull You Down

These days, people find it hard to imagine a life free from debt. Cars can't be without payment, houses without mortgage, and getting through college without acquiring a loan. And Americans now have $928 billion in credit-card debt. But can't we really live without debt?

One of the major barriers to winning is how we view debt. Most of the people who underwent the Total Money Makeover and decided to stop borrowing money have been ridiculed by friends and family. So many people believe that debt is good so anyone who turns their back on debt is assumed to be unintelligent and ignorant in finance. But if that's the case, why are there so many finance teachers who are broke?

Myth vs. Truth

To discover how the Debt Myth works, let's take a look at its sub-myths. If you find yourself defending the American way of borrowing money, calm down and try to finish these few pages.

Myth: You can use debt as a tool in building prosperity.

Truth: Debt can be considered a double-edged sword. It cuts for you but it can also cut into you. With debt, you can buy a car or a house, start a business, or go shopping without the need to wait. But debt is associated with lots of risks that they offset any benefit that could be gained through such debt.

Wealthy people don't rely on debt as much as we're made to believe. Out of the 400 wealthiest people in America, 300 believe that the best approach to build wealth is to stay away from debt. Millionaires became what they are by living on less than what they made and only spending what cash they had.

Myth: Lending money to relatives or friends is a good way to help them.

Truth: Lending money to relative or friends could only hurt or destroy your relationship.

Joan's relationship with one of her work best friends was ruined with a loan. That friend borrowed $50 from her and promised to return the money on payday. But she didn't and now avoided Joan. Debt enslaves the borrower to the lender and you alter relationships when you give a loan to your loved ones. The only way to get rid of the master-servant relationship is to forgive the debt. If you have it, you can give money to a friend who desperately needs it but lending money will only spoil relationship.

Myth: You can help a friend or relative by cosigning a loan.

Truth: If lenders are required to meet a quota and they can foresee with incredible accuracy the probability of a loan's going into default, denying your friend or relative a loan means that he or she is seen by lenders as a potential problem. And yet, so many Americans still cosign for somebody else every day.

Joe cosigned for a mobile home his brother acquired 15 years ago. Five years after the transaction, the home was repossessed and sold $16,000 less than what was owed. The bank tracked down Joe 10 years later and demanded its money. Joe was so angry that the bank could do that to him because he didn't have any idea what he signed up for, just like almost everyone else who agrees to do it.

Myth: Rent-to-Own, Payday Loans, and Cash Advance help people with low income to get ahead.

Truth: These rip-offs will only trap the lower-income people at the foot of the socioeconomic ladder. These types of loans have more than 100% interest rate. Take for example Payday Loan, which is the fastest-growing trash lender. If you write a $225 post-dated check, they will give you $200 cash. If the check is dated a week from now, the $25 service charge equates to more than 650% interest annually.

By using Tote-the-Note, Rent-to-Own, and Payday Loans, you allow yourself to be financially destroyed. If you want to be successful with money, avoid these kinds of businesses at all costs.

Myth: You can't avoid car payments because it's a way of life.

Truth: Most people think that keeping car payment throughout their lives is normal. So once they pay off a car, they get a new one. What they don't realize is that they missed the chance to save $495 monthly – the average car payment for over 64 months. If you invested this amount for 40 years on a mutual fund with 12% average, you would have $6 million by the time you retire.

If you save that $495 per month, you will have more than enough for a cash car. Your car may be junk but at least you are without debt. And that is a sign that you're on the right track.

Myth: A new car at 0% interest is a good deal.

Truth: Unless you're a millionaire, you can't afford a new car. 0% interest is not real. Cars lose 60% of their value in four years. If you buy a new car for $28,000 because you're after the warranty, the $17,000 of value you will lose over four years is too much for a warranty.

Myth: You must have a credit card to build your credit.

Truth: Bankers tell you that you should build your credit so that you can get more debt because that is how you will be able to acquire stuff. But you will only want to do that if you want your life to depend on credit cards, car payments, and student loans. With your Total Money Makeover, you won't be needing a credit card.

Myth: A credit card is required when renting a car, checking in to a hotel, or buying online.

Truth: You can do all that with a debit card. The only difference is that you should have the money in your debit card before paying for anything using it. And there are some businesses which don't accept debit cards. But that's very few.

Myth: Giving your teenager a credit card will teach him to be responsible with money.

Truth: The fact is that even before they get a job, 88% of graduating college students already has credit-card debts. And according to the American Bankruptcy Institute, 19% of people who filed for bankruptcy were students. Doing so will only make your teenager financially irresponsible.

Myth: If you consolidate your debts, you will only have one payment and save on interest.

Truth: Debt consolidation lowers the payment and interest rate because the term is usually extended. And the longer you are in debt, the more you pay the lenders.

Myth: If people stop borrowing money, the economy will collapse.

Truth: In the first few years, the economy will collapse. Because many people won't have actual money to spend. But in the long run, say 50 years, the economy would prosper, except bank and other lenders. Without payments, people would be able to save and spend, supporting a more stable economy.

Chapter 4: Money Myths: The (Non)Secrets of the Rich

Most of the myths about money involve lies about shortcut or security. The myths presented in this chapter developed from two basic issues: risk denial and easy wealth.

Risk denial could be a form of laziness when we don't want to exert an effort to realize that effort is required to win. Sometimes, it's a kind of submission when we are so beat up that we just settle for a poor solution. Other times, it's when we look for a false sense of security that is non-existent.

The second problem is the search for easy wealth. Shortcuts never provide us high quality. One of the oldest lies told in human history is the myth of quick and easy money.

Myth vs. Truth

Myth: It's okay to not start saving early for retirement because everything will be fine when that time comes.

Truth: Don't expect this government to take care of you when you get old. Taking care of your future is your job. Nothing will be fine unless you invest in your future.

Myth: Investing in gold will shelter you in case the economy collapses.

Truth: Sellers of gold as an investment convince potential investors that in a collapsed economy, gold will keep hold of its value. People buy into this idea and invest in gold because they are made to believe it will provide them security. But it's proven that gold is a lousy investment, and at best, only has a 4.4% rate of return. Gold will be useless if the economy collapses.

Myth: There are effective ways to get rich quickly, and working just three hours every week.

Truth: If people offer you something that is too good to be true, it is. A 500-to-1 return on your money is definitely a scam, and there's no way to get rich by working only three hours weekly. Don't fall for this and get away from these people.

Myth: If you want to retire with a fat pocket, buy Cash Value life insurance.

Truth: Cash Value is an insurance+savings package and over 70% of life insurance policies today are of this kind. Investing in life insurance isn't a wise decision because the returns are terrible.

Myth: Instead of renting, it's better to buy a mobile home or trailer.

Truth: A trailer you buy today for $25,000 will have a value of $8,000 after five years, and leave you with a debt of $22,000. The fastest way to own a house is renting the cheapest place you're willing to suffer through.

Myth: To protect yourself against inflation, prepay your funeral and your children's college expenses.

Truth: When you prepay for something, you're able to avoid price increase. And that price increase is your return of investment. The average price increase for tuition at national level is about 8%. This is equivalent to investing at 8%, which isn't bad. But mutual funds could offer 12% for a long period of time. When you prepay, you only put your money in somebody else's pocket.

Myth: AmeriDebt and other debt management companies will save you.

Truth: Debt management companies help you get lower interest rates and payments. But if you employ any of them, you'll be treated like someone who'd filed a Chapter 13 Bankruptcy when you try to get a loan. The other problem with using them is that they don't change your habits. They don't improve the way you handle money.

Myth: There's a kit you can buy to clean up your credit.

Truth: Unless the item is inaccurate, nothing can be taken off your credit report. These kits are scam. Kits that instruct you to get another Social Security number in order to get a brand new credit report will only lead you to jail.

Myth: You don't have to pay the debt if the divorce decree says your spouse has to pay for it.

Truth: The divorce judge can only order your spouse to pay a debt for you but it can't take your name off the debt. If debts don't get paid by your spouse, you must be prepared to pay.

Myth: It's easy to file for bankruptcy and start over.

Truth: Out of the many who have been through bankruptcy, only a few could say that it's a painless process. Bankruptcy stays on your credit report for life. Loan and many job applications inquire if you've ever filed for bankruptcy.

Myth: Using cash is an invitation to get robbed.

Truth: By using cash, you're forced to spend less because it hurts more to part with money that you actually have. Cash can also get you bargains. You're being robbed every time you don't use cash.

Myth: Many people can't afford insurance.

Truth: Be responsible and buy the right kinds of insurance that will cover life and death. As part of your Total Money Makeover, you must have Auto and Homeowner Insurance, Long-Term Disability, Life Insurance, Health Insurance, and Long-Term Care Insurance.

Myth: You'll die if you make a will.

Truth: If you die without a will, the state will have the power to dictate what happens to everything you own. The best gift you can give your loved ones is a will because it makes management of your estate easier.

Chapter 5: Two More Hurdles: Ignorance and Keeping Up with the Joneses

Denial, Debt Myths, and Money Myths are three main hindrances the keep you from being financially fit. But there are two more hurdles we must analyze before moving on to the proven plan.

Hurdle #1: Ignorance: No One Is Born Financially Smart

Ignorance about money doesn't mean lack of intelligence. It refers to lack of the competence to handle money. We were born without all the knowledge and skills we possess now. Therefore, financial know-how is also learned. But no one seems to teach us that.

It's easy to overcome ignorance. Confess without shame that you're not expert in financial matters, read everything in this book, and never stop learning more about money. The process is easy but you still have to spend time and energy to free yourself from ignorance. Instead of spending a lot of time picking out this year's vacation, pay more attention to your budget and 401k options instead.

Hurdle #2: Keeping Up with the Joneses: The Joneses Can't Do Math

We all feel the need to become part of a certain group and we do some insane things to fulfill our need for respect and approval. One of the most common things we do is buying unnecessary stuff we couldn't really afford to show others that we're wealthy. But real millionaires don't have the things most people think they do. Instead of keeping up with the expectations of friends and family, they are motivated by the goal of financial security.

For the past seven years, Sara and Bob have been making $93,000 annually. Combining their home mortgage, car payments, home equity loan, credit-card debts, student loan, and expenses for their travel and high-fashion clothes, these two have a negative net worth. Still, they look good and everyone thinks that they're doing well. The Joneses, it turns out, are broke.

A major change is necessary for a money breakthrough. But resistance is real. Everyone likes nice houses and cars and selling them would be painful. No one would like to admit to everyone they have impressed that they are fake. It would take a lot of courage to be real.

Before you can proceed with your real plan to financial

fitness, you must recognize what your weak spot is. It could be your addiction to high fashion clothes, giving to your grown-up kids, or a failing business that must be closed. Until you identify this, you'll always be likely to make financial stupidity on this matter.

Past the Obstacle Course and Up the Mountain

Your journey through Total Money Makeover is like an obstacle course. It requires you to break through denial, climb over Debt and Money Myths, toil through ignorance, and stop keeping up with the Joneses. But this obstacle course is only part of the journey.

You need to climb a mountain, and this will be nearly impossible if you're still struggling with any of the five obstacles. The goal of this climb may be far, but there's a distinct and clear path that will lead you to the top.

Chapter 6: Save $1,000 Fast: Walk Before You Run

The key to doing anything, be it financial or not, is to take one tiny step at a time. To walk through your Total Money Makeover, you will be taking Baby Steps. Tens of thousands have gone along this system and they were able to achieve their goals.

Eating an Elephant Gives You Energy

Doing everything at once will only lead to failure. If you want to do something, complete the first step before moving on to the next.

Baby Steps works because it gives you the ability to focus. If you do everything at once, your effort will be diluted. It will take so much time to finish what you've started. That will make you feel like you're not accomplishing anything and soon you will lose the motivation and energy to complete your task of money management.

With Baby Steps, you're also able to prioritize. Unless done in order, the proven plan to fiscal fitness won't work. You have to walk before doing a 10-mile run. Before starting the Baby

Steps, you must work on your patience. There's no shortcut and if you make a jump to any step ahead, you're less likely to win.

YOU, Inc.

Before learning how to save $1,000 fast, you must set up a monthly budget first and write it down. If your work for a company called YOU, Inc. was to manage money, would it fire you with the way you manage your personal money now? Having a written monthly budget gives you a goal. And without something to aim at, you'll hit nothing. For most of us, succeeding on a big scale only requires well-defined, written goals.

Prepare a new budget each month. Your income and outgo must have zero difference. Match your monthly income with the month's bills, debt payments, and savings. If you're married, you and your spouse must agree on the budget. If you can't work together, it will be impossible to win. If you'd need to change anything mid-month because of some emergency, you should only do it if both of you agree and make sure that you still balance your budget.

One more thing you must do before taking the Baby Steps is to be current with all your payment. If you're far behind, prioritize necessities such as basic food and utilities before catching up on student loans and credit cards.

Baby Step One: Save $1,000 Cash as a Starter Emergency Fund

According to *Money* magazine, a major negative event will occur to 78% of us in a given 10-year period. This shouldn't be a surprise and you must be ready by having an emergency fund.

Most Americans use credit cards to cover many things they think are emergencies like Christmas presents, car repairs, and clothes for kids. None of these are emergencies and should be included in your budget. Whether real or perceived, emergencies shouldn't be covered with credit cards. The dependence on it must be broken.

If your annual income is below $20,000, your beginner fund can be $500. If it's above that, you must be able to save $1,000 quick. Your makeover starts with the emergency fund and not with the debt because most people abandon their journey when emergency strikes. Your beginner fund will keep emergencies from turning into another debt.

This step should be completed in less than a month. Work extra hours or have a garage sale. Do everything to accomplish this task fast. And when you do, hide the $1,000. Keep it handy and it will get spent. If you put the money in a savings account, don't attach it to your checking account.

If you already have $1,000 in a Certificate of Deposit with penalties, mutual funds, savings bonds, checking, stocks, or bonds, take it out. Your emergency fund should be liquid. All the extra money you have will be used in the second step.

If you're already on Step 2 and you used part of your emergency fund, return to the first step and replenish your $1,000. Only then can you go back to Step 2. If you skip it, you may find yourself borrowing money again to cover a real emergency.

Chapter 7: The Debt Snowball: Lose Weight Fast, Really

Your income is your greatest wealth-building tool. And in order to build and preserve wealth, you must gain full control of your income.

Identify the Enemy

Without any payments, it's easy to build wealth. And when you identify your enemy, you'll be able to win your battle. Getting rid of debt enables people to make huge steps toward their first million.

A typical American earns a net of $3,350 per month. $1,995 of it goes to payments for house, cars, student loan, credit card, and personal loans. If he has no payments, he would be able to invest that money and become a cash mutual-fund millionaire in just 15 years.

You may now be convinced that you can be wealthy if you can get yourself out of debt. And there's a foolproof way to do it. It's very difficult and average people won't do it but you're not one of them. This step is the toughest and it will require the most effort and sacrifice. But it will be worth it.

Baby Step Two: Start the Debt Snowball

Debt Snowball is the way you will pay off debt. List all your debts except your home, starting with the smallest balance or payoff. If two debts have equal payoffs, list the one with higher interest rate first. Paying off the smaller one first is faster and the higher chance for you staying with the plan. The only time you should pay the larger debts sooner is during an emergency like when the IRS is after you or if there's a risk of foreclosure.

After listing all your debts, pay the minimum on each debt but every dollar you find in your budget must go to the smallest debt. Once it's fully paid, add the money for that debt to any extra you can find to the next smallest debt. And when it's paid off, add the money for the first two along with any extra to pay for debt number three. Keep doing it until you pay all your debts.

The Elements of Making It Work

The major elements that make the Debt Snowball work are using a written budget, getting current with all your payment before starting, paying off smallest debt first, sacrifice, and most importantly, focused intensity. Thinking of sort of giving the Debt Snowball a try won't work. Focused intensity is required if you want to win.

Remember that when you're working on the Debt Snowball, avoid borrowing money at any circumstance. Doing so will only change the names of lenders on your list. Cut up you credit cards even before paying them off.

How to Get the Snowball Rolling

For some people, getting the Debt Snowball to roll is difficult. When doing their budget, there's not even enough for minimum payments. The solution to this is making a sacrifice. An example is selling stuff you barely use. You can also sell big things like the car with the most debt on it. But don't sell your house unless it's taking more than 45% of your take-home-pay. Except for the house, a good rule of thumb for things is that if you can't pay-off for that item in 18 to 20 months, you should sell it. If you don't want to sell, find ways to increase your income like working more hours or taking an extra job.

What About Saving for Retirement While the Snowball's Rolling?

Even if you're company is matching 100% of your 401k contributions, if you're really focused on becoming debt-free and you've done everything but still can't get the snowball rolling, you should stop saving for retirement. The power of quick wins is more significant than the match to your makeover in the long term.

Second Mortgages, Business Debt, and Rental Property Mortgages

If you have a second mortgage, you should include it in the Debt Snowball if it's less than half your gross annual income. Otherwise, you'll get to it in a different step. And if you can lower the interest rates, consider refinancing your two mortgages.

Small-business loans which are personally guaranteed are considered personal debts and should be included in the Debt Snowball. But if it's more than 50% of your home mortgage or gross annual income, pay it off later. Mortgages on rental properties should also be delayed.

Chapter 8: Finish the Emergency Fund: Kick Murphy Out

Most focused participants of the Makeover will reach the third step with $1,000 and only home mortgage in 18 to 20 months.

Baby Step Three: Finish the Emergency Fund

Your emergency fund should cover expenses for three to six months. A fully funded one ranges from $5,000 to $25,000. Emergencies will happen and people make the biggest mistake of borrowing during this event. 56% of Americans said they'd use a credit card in bad times. It's not difficult but it's a stupid move. And 49% have savings enough for only a month's expenses.

Before using your emergency fund, think through and identify if you're facing a real emergency.

The Emergency Fund Must Be Easy to Access

Make sure to keep your emergency fund in something easy to get to and with no penalties. Don't put your emergency money in mutual funds because these are designed for long-term investing and you'll just be tempted to borrow instead of cashing in when the market is down. And unless you get a "quick-release" allowing one withdrawal over a certain period without penalty, don't put your emergency fund in Certificates of Deposit. A no-penalty account with Money Market with full checkwriting privileges is the best choice for your emergency fund.

Keep in mind that the goal of having an emergency fund is not to build wealth but to protect you from the bad times and keep problems from turning into debts.

How Big?

The amount in your emergency fund will depend on your situation. The riskier it is, the bigger your fund must be. If you're self-employed, single, or a one-income household, the fund must be able to cover you for six months. The same goes if you have an unstable job or there are chronic medical issues in your household.

If your job is stable and everyone is healthy, you have the option to have money enough only for three months. Men and women usually have different opinion with this matter. Because this isn't just for actual protection but for peace of mind as well, the spouse wanting a higher amount wins.

Gender and Emergencies

It's true that genders view the emergency fund in different

ways. In general, most men don't understand how money just sitting there creates security. Meanwhile, women consider life insurance and emergency fund as the best parts of their Makeover.

Guys, women are better-wired when it comes to this matter. Therefore, create an emergency fund even you don't understand it.

An Emergency Fund Can Turn Crises into Inconveniences

As your Makeover improves your money habit, you'll have to rely on your emergency fund less and less. You'll have fewer things that your monthly budget can't afford. And as you make progress on your Makeover, you'll have better health and disability insurance and larger budget so there'll be fewer things that must be covered by your emergency fund.

If You Don't Own a Home

If you haven't bought a house yet, don't buy one or even start saving for downpayment until you're done with Step 3. And while taking the 15-year fixed-rate mortgage is okay, the 100% down plan is still a lot better. Many people worry about having a home but a house might feel like a curse for those who rushed into buying one.

Chapter 9: Maximize Retirement Investing: Be Financially Healthy for Life

When working on your Total Money Makeover, focused intensity is only mandatory to get to the wealth steps. Maintenance of your wealth will require less effort if you don't forget the principles that got you there. But remember that you still can lose your fiscal fitness.

Now that you've paid your debts and completed your emergency fund, it's time for you to invest.

What Retirement Isn't

In the context of our Makeover, retirement means having enough money so that work is only an option. You can choose to make music or be with your grandkids; anything that gives you joy. The goal of investing for retirement should be security.

While you must not wait until you reach the golden age to do the things that you love, money still matters. You must have a plan if you want to grow old with dignity.

Baby Step Four: Invest 15% of Your Income in Retirement

Note that when you reach Step 4, the only payment that you have should be house and you have thousands of dollars of savings. So even if your income is below average, investing heavily should be easy.

15% of your gross income should be invested toward retirement; no more, no less. If you have extra, that will be saved for paying off your house early and your kids' college. And if you're struggling to allot 15% because you want to prioritize college degree and a fully paid house, remember that those two won't take care of you when you get old.

When computing the 15%, exclude company matches and your potential Social Security benefits.

Your Tool Is Mutual Funds

When investing money for more than five years, growth-stock mutual funds are the best choice. In the stock market's history, 97% of 5-year periods made money for the 10-year periods, 100% did. When choosing mutual funds, select those with good track record for five to ten years. Don't look at records less than five years because mutual funds are horrible short-term investments.

Start investing where you have a match. Your next priority should be Roth IRA, which allows most people to invest a maximum of $5,000 annually, tax-free. If you're still investing less than 15% of your annual gross income, go back to SEPPs, 401ks, 403bs, or 457s.

What It Will Take to Retire

The idea is for you to be able to live off of 8% of your nest egg annually. The nest egg earns 12% per year so the other 4% covers inflation. To compute how much nest egg you need, determine the annual income you wish to retire on and divide it by 8%. The result will be your nest egg. The amount you need to save each month is the nest egg multiplied by a factor applicable to you. Select from the table below.

Age	Years to Save	Factor
25	40	0.000286
30	35	0.000436
35	30	0.000671
40	25	0.001051
45	20	0.001698
50	15	0.002890
55	10	0.005466
60	5	0.013610

If you're in your 40s and thinking that it's too late for you to invest, it isn't. There's nothing we can do about the time that has passed. So start investing right now because you have no other option.

Remember that the goal of this step is not to get rich quick. You must be consistently and systematically investing over time if you want to get wealthy. And if you don't prioritize investing, you're doomed to work all your life because you have to.

Chapter 10: College Funding: Make Sure the Kids Are Fit Too

A degree in college is important. Having a solid education will add quality to career and adult life.

Understand the Purpose of a College Education Before You Fund It

Before sending off your kids to the most expensive school, understand that a college degree does not guarantee a job, wealth or success. If you expect that it will, be prepared for a letdown especially when your graduate moves back in with you. Knowledge gained through college will only work for a person if he mixes it with attitude, hard work, vision, perseverance, and character.

Dave's Rules for College

Conduct extensive research on the cost of going to college. Find out and compare how much it costs to go to your old college, the big and small state schools in your area, and small private colleges. Where you got your degree doesn't matter much in many fields and careers.

First rule: pay with cash. Second rule: if you have cash or scholarship, go to college. And never use a college degree as an excuse for you to go into debt. The average student-loan debt of graduates is $15,000. Much of these didn't go to actual college expenses but to apartment rent and off-campus dining. Debt wasn't required to get the degree but to look good while attending school.

Baby Step Five: Save for College

While almost everyone thinks that saving for college is necessary, only a few actually do save money. 39% of Americans have nothing saved for their kids' college education and only 9% use college savings funds. This is hardly a surprise when most of us are in debt and don't even have emergency funds.

ESAs and 529s

The average inflation of tuition is 8% so baby life insurance and savings bonds which average less than 8% won't work. Prepaying college tuition isn't so bad but there are much better options.

An Educational Savings Account (ESA) funded in a growth-stock mutual fund grows tax-free when allotted for college education. If your annual household income is less than $220,000, ESA allows you to invest $2,000 annually per child.

If you start from birth with ESA averaging 12%, you would have $126,000 by the time your kid is 18.

If you want something more than ESA or your household income is above the cut-off, you may want to take a look at a 529 plan. While most of these state plans let you use the money for college, you should choose among its several types wisely. The popular life phase plan performs poorly. While the fixed portfolio plan performs better but allows you less control of your money. If you're going for a 529, choose a flexible plan which lets you move your investment with mutual funds in the Fidelity, Vanguard, or American Funds Group.

To have enough for higher education, determine how much your college of choice costs per year and multiply it by four. That should be your college nest egg. And to determine how much you should save per month, multiply the nest egg by a factor you can choose from the table below.

Child's Age	Years to Save	Factor
0	18	0.002083
2	16	0.002583
4	14	0.003247
6	12	0.004158
8	10	0.005466
10	8	0.007470
12	6	0.010867
14	4	0.017746

Getting Creative When You Don't Have Much Time

If you have less than four years because you started late in your Makeover, plan on sending your kid to a cheaper institution where they could live on campus and dine at the cafeteria. You can also have your kid look into work-study programs which some companies are offering. Also consider what the military or the National Guard could offer, although this isn't for everyone.

If you're in school and you already have a loan or you don't want one, consider programs for under-served areas where the government will pay off your loan or pay for school. This is usually offered for law and medicine courses. Lastly, other than saving, you can look for scholarships, the lists of which can be bought online. These are small dollar amounts coming from organizations but you could apply and be accepted in several, which could pay you enough to go to college for free.

Chapter 11: Pay Off the Home Mortgage: Be Ultrafit

Reaching this point, you should have no more debts except for the house, you've completed your emergency fund, you're investing 15% of your income for retirement, and you have a separate investment for your kids' education. By now, you are part of the top 10% of Americans because you have a plan and some wealth.

But you're still not out of danger. You may be tempted to settle for "Good Enough." Don't. All those who chose to stop at this point regretted their decision.

Baby Step Six: Pay Off Your Home Mortgage

The goal of this step is to make you completely debt-free. To most people, paying off the mortgage is like creating wings and flying to the moon – impossible. That's because they have lost their hope of becoming debt-free. And they believe all the myths about mortgage. So, we must dispel some more of them.

Myth: Keep your home mortgage and take advantage of tax deduction.

Truth: If your home payment is $900 with an interest option of $830, the approximately $10,000 of interest you've paid for a year generates a tax deduction. If you don't have that debt, you will lose the tax deduction on you would have to pay IRS $3,000 if you're in the 30% bracket. Would you rather pay the IRS $3,000 in taxes or the bank $10,000 in interest?

Myth: Borrowing all you can on your home to invest the money and take advantage of great interest rates is a wise decision.

Truth: Some Americans are told to borrow at about 8% and use the money borrowed on their home to invest on mutual funds averaging 12% to make an easy 4%. If you borrow $100,000, you will have to pay the bank $8,000 and you will make $12,000 out of your investment, netting $4,000. But you will have to pay taxes. And depending on the tax rate, your actual earnings will be between $400 and $1,600.

Likewise, remember that you're more at risk if you have debts. During the 2008-09 recession, everyone who lost their houses to foreclosure had a mortgage.

Myth: Choose a 30-year mortgage and swear to pay it like a 15-year so you'll have a wiggle room if something bad happens.

Truth: According to FDIC, 97.3% of borrowers don't

systematically pay more than their mortgage. If your house costs $250,000, you will only have to add $550 monthly and save about $150,000 at 7% interest rate. It will also save you from 15 more years of bondage.

Myth: Instead of having an emergency fund, take a home-equity loan.

Truth: Home-equity loans are dangerous and many of them result to foreclosures. Remember that the last thing you want during emergencies is debt. If you're in a real emergency situation and you borrow tens of thousands of dollars against your house, you'll probably lose your house.

Myth: Paying cash for a house is impossible.

Truth: Paying cash for a house is possible if you are willing to make certain sacrifices in your lifestyle, never borrow money, and live on next to nothing.

But if you really can't pay cash, never take greater than a 15-year fixed-rate loan and payment should never be more than 20% of your take-home pay.

Chapter 12: Build Wealth Like Crazy: Arnold Schwarzedollar, Mr. Universe of Money

By the time you reach Step 7, you're already part of the top 2% of Americans. You're completely debt-free, your retirement is secured, and you've regained control of your life and your income.

Baby Step Seven: Build Wealth

Your money has three good uses. It's good for fun, to invest, and to give. So one day if you wake up with $18 million, do all of these things. And even when you're still working on the steps to wealth, you should already be doing these.

Yes, We Get to Have Fun

Should anyone wear a watch that costs tens of thousands of dollar, drive a brand-new luxury car, or live in a million-dollar home? Absolutely. But only if he could really afford those things.

Building wealth that will let you have fun is one of the reasons for doing a Makeover. When you have millions of dollars, you can afford to buy large diamond rings, a brand new card, and take your family on a week-long cruise. Doing these things would hardly affect your money position and you'll be able to enjoy guilt-free.

Investing Is How We Keep on Winning

Investing is a big part of what makes and keeps you wealthy. But when doing this, remember that there'll be times when you can be up and sometimes you can get behind. When the market fluctuates, don't be scared because if you have quality investments, they will come back. Never cash everything out when the market is down.

Unless you have more than $10 million, keep away from extremely complex investments. Debt-free real estate and simple mutual funds are enough for now.

Management of your money is your responsibility. But surround yourself with a team of people who are smarter than you and have the heart of a teach. A good CPA or tax expert, estate-planning attorney, insurance and investment pros, and a realtor are essential team members.

There's a Subsection B within Step 7. The second milestone in your wealth-building is the Pinnacle Point – the point at which your money is making more than you do. You'll still have to manage and direct what you have but you'll see that wealth comes to you on its own. This is when you're officially wealthy.

Giving Is the Biggest Reward of the Entire Workout

Fun and investing are good, but eventually they will lose their appeal. Giving is probably the most fun you'll have with money. And one of the things that healthy millionaires share is their love of giving.

Chapter 13: Live Like No One Else

When you started this book, you were fiscally unfit. But because the Total Money Makeover plan works, you'll be wealthy over the next 20 to 40 years. And there's a big problem. When you've tasted wealth, there's a chance of you becoming enamored to it. We may start worshipping money.

False Cents of Security

If your wealth gives you the idea that you're some big deal because of the money that you have, you've totally missed the point of this Makeover. And you're no more free than a debt-ridden person.

Because this book is about wealth-building, you might think that it advocates the idea that owning stuff is the key to happiness and emotional well-being. On the contrary, there is much danger to having enormous wealth. And that is materialism. In the book *Money, Possessions, and Eternity*, Randy Alcorn said that by expecting stuff to do things they're not intended to do, people end up feeling depressed and even suicidal.

Good things will only result from your Makeover if you

understand that wealth isn't the answer to life's questions. And while wealth is fun, there's great responsibility attached to it.

Wealth will not necessarily change you but make you more of what you currently are. If a jerk gets rich, he'll be the king of jerks. If you're generous and kind, your wealth will allow you to spread more of your generosity and kindness.

The LOVE of Money, Not Money, Is the Root of All Evil

Certain religious and political groups have made a decision that wealth is evil. They must have forgotten that many biblical and historical heroes are of great wealth. This negativity seems to justify financial mediocrity. Money is not evil, and wealthy people are not evil by virtue of their money.

If you're someone who is good, it's your responsibility to acquire riches so you can do with them things that bring good to mankind. If you believe that wealth is evil, you're leaving all the riches to evil people by default. Your duty is to get wealth and keep money away from the bad ones because as a good person, you'll do good with it.

Meet The Winners of The Total Money Makeover Challenge

During the first publication of The Total Money Makeover, a contest was started to determine who could change their financial position the most within six months. Out of hundreds who sent in their entries, ten finalists were chosen and brought to the Bahamas. During that trip, one family was awarded with the $50,000 grand prize. Here's their story.

Before starting their Makeover, Chance and Kimberly Morrow had a debt of more than $56,000, with an income of $35,000. Their monthly payments were at least $1,200. A financial planner told them that it would take 40 years to pay off their debt.

Upon listening to The Dave Ramsey Show, they realized that there's a plan that could work. That Christmas, instead of buying a fancy tree, they used Chance's bonus check of about $1,000 for Baby Step 1. They set a goal to pay off $10,000 that first year. They stopped using their credit cards, lived on a written budget, cut every expense they could, worked overtime, took a second job, and had garage sales. By next Christmas, they were able to pay off $14,000.

Then they decided to sell their house. It made them debt-free and completed their six-month emergency fund. That's about the time they got a call informing them they're finalists in The Challenge.

They donated part of the prize money to their church. They took their kids on a trip and used the rest of the money toward a downpayment on a house. Four years later, they were completely debt-free and with a new house. That was 36 years earlier than what their financial planner projected.

Conclusion

Building wealth is more about a person's behavior than their knowledge about money. Many people are stuck with debts because they believe it's a normal part of life and they don't see that their money-spending habits are unhealthy. People are not changing their spending habits and thus their life because they don't think there's any problem.

Debt shouldn't be a part of life. And borrowed money must never be considered a tool for building wealth. When you go through the Total Money Makeover, you realize that you can live without relying on credit cards and having payments. You understand the importance of investing and there's no shortcut in building wealth. You know that by living the way most people don't, you'll be able to live the way most people can't.

The first step of saving $1,000 as your emergency fund is also a way of learning to do things with small steps. And with smaller and achievable goals, you're able to win little victories that motivate you to continue your journey. And having an emergency fund will keep you from incurring more debts if something bad happens while you work on paying off your debts.

Debt Snowball is the way you pay off your debt systematically. You start with paying the smallest ones and by the time you get to the huge debts, which could be overwhelming if not done in a systematic way, you find that you can pay more than you think you could. And most people are able to pay off all their debts (except the house) in just 20 months.

A complete emergency fund must cover three to six months of living expenses. You must put this fund where you can have easy access to it. And remember that this money is only for emergency and will not be used to build your wealth. Having a complete emergency fund can turn real emergencies into mere inconveniences.

To have a comfortable retirement, you must prepare for it. You should invest 15% of your gross income toward retirement. And when investing long-term, your best bet is mutual funds which average 12%.

If you're already investing for retirement and you have extra, that money would be used for your kids' education and paying off the house. When planning for college, research about the cost of sending your kids to different schools. Remember that in most fields and careers, where you got your degree doesn't matter much. A degree is important but it's unwise to go into debt just so you could send you kids to an expensive school.

If you don't have a house yet, save until you could pay for it in cash. But if you really want to have a house sooner, you should never go beyond 15 years. It will save you a lot of money and keep you from years of bondage.

When you've built your wealth, remember that your money should be used for having fun, investing, and giving. And when your money makes more than you do, that's when you're officially wealthy.

About the Author

Dave Ramsey is the Author of *More Than Enough* and *Financial Peace*. His radio program, *The Dave Ramsey Show*, is heard on more than 450 radio stations across the U.S. and transmits financial advice to nearly 4.5 million listeners weekly.

FREE BONUSES

P.S. Is it okay if we overdeliver?

Here at Readtrepreneur Publishing, we believe in overdelivering way beyond our reader's expectations. Is it okay if we overdeliver?

Here's the deal, we're going to give you an extremely condensed PDF summary of the book which you've just read and much more…

What's the catch? We need to trust you… You see, we want to overdeliver and in order for us to do that, we've to trust our reader to keep this bonus a secret to themselves? Why? Because we don't want people to be getting our exclusive PDF summaries even without buying our books itself. Unethical, right?

Ok. Are you ready?

Firstly, remember that your book is code: **"READ119"**.

Next, visit this link: **http://bit.ly/exclusivepdfs**

Everything else will be self explanatory after you've visited: **http://bit.ly/exclusivepdfs.**

We hope you'll enjoy our free bonuses as much as we enjoyed preparing it for you!

Summary:

The Untethered Soul

By: Michael A. Singer

Proudly Brought to you by:

READTREPRENEUR
— WORLD'S BEST BOOK SUMMARIES —

Text Copyright © Readtrepreneur

All rights reserved. No part of this guide may be reproduced in any form without permission in writing from the publisher except in the case of brief quotations embodied in critical articles or reviews.

Legal & Disclaimer

The information contained in this book is not designed to replace or take the place of any form of medicine or professional medical advice. The information in this book has been provided for educational and entertainment purposes only.

The information contained in this book has been compiled from sources deemed reliable, and it is accurate to the best of the Author's knowledge; however, the Author cannot guarantee its accuracy and validity and cannot be held liable for any errors or omissions. Changes are periodically made to this book. You must consult your doctor or get professional medical advice before using any of the suggested remedies, techniques, or information in this book. Images used in this book are not the same as of that of the actual book. This is a totally separate and different entity from that of the original book titled: "The Untethered Soul: The Journey Beyond Yourself".

Upon using the information contained in this book, you agree to hold harmless the Author from and against any damages, costs, and expenses, including any legal fees potentially resulting from the application of any of the information provided by this guide. This disclaimer applies to any damages or injury caused by the use and application, whether directly or indirectly, of any advice or information presented, whether for breach of contract, tort, negligence, personal injury, criminal intent, or under any other cause of action.

You agree to accept all risks of using the information presented inside this book. You need to consult a professional medical practitioner in order to ensure you are both able and healthy enough to participate in this program.

Table of Contents

Acknowledgments 83

Introduction (The Book at a Glance) 84

FREE BONUSES 87

PART I: 89

Awakening Consciousness 89

Chapter 1. The Voice Inside Your Head 90

Chapter 2. Your Inner Roommate 93

Chapter 3. Who Are You? 96

Chapter 4. The Lucid Self 99

PART II: 102

Experiencing Energy 102

Chapter 5. Infinite Energy 103

Chapter 6. The Secrets of the Spiritual Heart 106

Chapter 7. Transcending the Tendency to Close 109

Part III: 112

Freeing Yourself 112

Chapter 8. Let Go Now or Fall 113

Chapter 9. Removing Your Inner Thorn 116

Chapter 10. Stealing Freedom for Your Soul 119

Chapter 11. Pain, the Price of Freedom 122

Part IV: 125

Going Beyond 125

Chapter 12. Taking Down the Walls 126

Chapter 13. Far, Far Beyond 129

Chapter 14. Letting Go of False Solidity 132

Part V: 135

Living Life 135

Chapter 15. The Path of Unconditional Happiness
.... 136

Chapter 16. The Spiritual Path of Nonresistance 139

Chapter 17. Contemplating Death 142

Chapter 18. The Secret of the Middle Way 144

Chapter 19. The Loving Eyes of God 146

Conclusion **149**

FREE BONUSES **152**

Acknowledgments

Years ago, Linda Bean transcribed some of Michael's lectures and she encouraged him to publish a book. She worked through archived materials and soon enough, Michael began writing. Linda's dedication and commitment to this piece of work are highly appreciated.

The moment Michael started writing, Karen Entner helped him by arranging materials, coming up with content suggestions, as well as keeping the manuscript. They worked together in editing several versions until every word brought a feeling of peace to his mind, heart, and soul. Karen's heartfelt work and dedication are profoundly appreciated and the publication of Michael's book was a lifelong dream of hers.

Introduction (The Book at a Glance)

How well do you really know yourself? It's not even enough to simply know your name or the place where you live. Your self is actually bigger than what you thought you know. To understand this, you must be willing to take the step to go deeper and further within the depths of your inner being. You'll be surprised to find that life still has full of mysteries that are yet to be realized.

Freud, who is known to be the father of psychology, divided the self or psyche into three different parts: the id, ego, and superego. He considered the id to be our fundamental, animal nature. The superego acts as the method of judgment, which society has established within us. The ego is what represents us to the world outside that struggles to keep the balance between the forces of id and superego.

Most of the time, we perceive that things aren't always as simple as they appear. If we have the courage to look beyond the surface of "self," many questions start to come up that a lot of people would prefer not to ask.

In the next chapters of this book, we'll take on the journey in exploring our "self." However, we'll set our path in a different way. We won't be needing the sentiments of the well-known philosophers, or the masters in psychology. There will be no arguments, no religious views to choose, or other people's opinions to seek. Instead, we'll turn to the only source with a great firsthand knowledge on the matter. The kind of expert that has been gathering data on every moment of everyday life to provide answers to the questions. It is no other than you.

Your views and opinions on the subject are not necessary. Only your innate experience of what it's like to be you is what's important. Your knowledge is not what this book is after, but your direct experience. Failure is not an option here because your "self" is what you are all the time and in every place. Your sense of "self" just needs to be sorted out. Besides, it can become quite confusing in there.

This book consists of chapters, which simply mirrors the way you see your "self" in different points of view. Although this is an inner journey, it will rely on every detail of your life. The only thing that's needed is your willingness to sincerely look at yourself in the most natural and spontaneous way.

As you go through every page of this book, you'll find that you know more about yourself in terms of extremely complex subjects. The truth is, you already know how to find yourself, you just got distracted. Once you refocused, you'll realize that you also have the ability to free yourself. It's completely up to you. Once your inner journey is complete, you'll no longer have any reason to be confused, or to blame other people. You'll know what you need to do. You'll have a great sense of respect for who you really are.

FREE BONUSES

P.S. Is it okay if we overdeliver?

Here at Readtrepreneur Publishing, we believe in overdelivering way beyond our reader's expectations. Is it okay if we overdeliver?

Here's the deal, we're going to give you an extremely condensed PDF summary of the book which you've just read and much more…

What's the catch? We need to trust you… You see, we want to overdeliver and in order for us to do that, we've to trust our reader to keep this bonus a secret to themselves? Why? Because we don't want people to be getting our exclusive PDF summaries even without buying our books itself. Unethical, right?

Ok. Are you ready?

Firstly, remember that your book is code:
"READ120".

Next, visit this link: **http://bit.ly/exclusivepdfs**

Everything else will be self explanatory after you've visited: **http://bit.ly/exclusivepdfs.**

We hope you'll enjoy our free bonuses as much as we enjoyed preparing it for you!

PART I:

Awakening Consciousness

Chapter 1. The Voice Inside Your Head

There's always mental chatter happening inside the head. It never stops. It just goes on and on all day. Do you ever wonder why your mind talks endlessly?

Try taking a step back and analyze this voice. Be a little more familiar with it. Don't be too objective. Step away and watch how it talks. Notice that it grabs both parts of the conversation. You'll hear internal dialogue even when you're driving or trying to get some sleep. The problem is in the following: you tolerate it, that's why you become restless.

If you take some time to observe this voice, you'll immediately notice that not once does it ever shut up. It simply talks when left alone. It's like seeing someone who's walking and talking to his lone self.

You're the one who's both talking and listening at the same time. You even argue with this voice and you have no idea who will win the argument. It doesn't stay silent even when it's wrong.

In order to liberate yourself from the mental chatter, picture it like a vocalizing mechanism. It makes you think like there's someone else in there who's speaking to you. Don't identify what it says. If you hear it, it's clearly not you.

What's more important in terms of true growth is understanding that you're not the mind's voice. You're just the one hearing it. You can undergo many changes in life to try and find yourself, but none of these voices or personality aspects is the real you.

You'll realize that most of the things the voice tells you are meaningless. As a matter of fact, life will play out based on the forces that are beyond your control. It doesn't matter what the mind tells you about it. Life will continue to happen. Your thoughts can't influence anyone or anything, but you. The real cause of the problem is the disruption, which the mind creates about life.

Why, then, does it exist? There's actually an energy buildup inside your head that has to be unleashed, like when you're nervous or angry. Talking releases that energy.

The alternate realm that you can control is your inner world. The world outside just continues to move on with its laws. However, when the mental voice describes various external things to you, all your thoughts intermix and affect the way you experience the world. What you're really experiencing is a personal representation of the world based on you. This psychological manipulation lets you guard reality. In the world of thoughts, you can always do something to direct the experience.

Once you surpass the piece of you that's not okay, it's where real personal growth begins. Being aware that you're observing the voice while it talks is like standing at the entrance of a wonderful inner journey. If used well, it can truly lead to a genuine spiritual awakening.

Chapter 2. Your Inner Roommate

You can experience inner growth when you finally understand that you'll only feel at peace and contented when you no longer think about yourself. The "I" inside you is always facing different problems. These problems just keep on coming, one after the other.

You're never going to have a problem-free life, especially if the inner part of you has to deal with a lot of problems. Instead of asking what to do about it, try finding which part of you is troubled. If you wish to obtain peace in the midst of all your problems, you must try to figure out why a certain situation is considered a problem to you.

If you're angry, look inside you and notice which is the troubled part. If you can spot it, you're not it. It's always better to maintain unbiased recognition of the internal problem than to let yourself get lost in the outside situation. This is how you can distinguish a person who's spiritually-minded from a worldly one. A worldly person thinks that the outside world can solve his inner problems. If he can change things around him, then everything will be okay. However, to obtain real inner freedom, learn to observe your problems objectively rather than losing yourself in them. If you're angry, scared, or anxious, you won't be able to handle a situation well. You need to control your reaction first.

Rearranging things outside of you is not really a means to solve your problems. The only way is to go deeper and free that part of yourself that appears to have plenty of problems with the real world.

Your own being has a part that can separate itself from your personal melodrama. Simply be mindful of what you feel. You're the one inside who notices these things. You'll find that you're looking at someone's strong and weak aspects of personality. It's like having another person with you, like a "roommate," except that it won't even cooperate whenever you seek silence. It can easily mess everything up without giving you a notice. As soon as you realize this, you can be on your way to an actual transformation.

Once you've truly made an effort to practice being more aware and self-observant, you'll find that you can only get rid of your mental voice once you've decided that you truly want to eliminate it. As soon as you make that decision to let yourself be free of it, you're all set for the techniques and teachings. In time, you'll learn that you need to put a gap between you and your mind. You can accomplish this by setting your life paths when you're unclouded and not allowing yourself to be discouraged by the mind. Push your will to be more powerful than your habit of paying attention to that mental chatter. This is how you can reclaim your life.

Chapter 3. Who Are You?

Ramana Maharshi, a great teacher when it comes to yogic tradition, once said that to gain inner freedom, a person must sincerely and continuously ask "Who am I?" Whenever people try to ask you, "Who are you?" and you think about it, you'll realize that you've never even asked that specific question your whole life and actually meant it.

It's effortless to notice that you're different from the things you always look at. You are the subject that's examining the objects. It's easy to generalize by stating that if you're the one who's watching something, then it means that something isn't you. You know right away that the world outside isn't *you*. You're someone on the inside who's looking out, watching the world.

Still, the big question is about who you really are. Where could you possibly be if you're not on the outside world along with everything? If you pay attention, you'll know that you're still in there coming across feelings and emotions even if everything on the outside has disappeared. You're the one who's experiencing the inside sentiments and the outer world at the same time. The objects from both worlds take on one another to get your attention. Eventually, you'll understand that the stream of inner feelings and the outside world are continuously coming and going. However, it's you who remains aware of everything that passes right in front you. You're the one who experiences all of it.

Luckily, you know that you still exist even without your thoughts. For instance, when you meditate deeply, your thoughts are silent. You're just conscious that there aren't any thoughts bothering you. If you're inside going through the quietness that takes place once your thoughts break off, then your existence does not depend on thinking.

Thoughts can take a pause or get exceedingly loud. If you're aware that they exist, can't you find a way to eliminate them? Again, you're not your inner thoughts. You're just aware of them.

When the question, "Who am I?" starts be entirely important, you begin to deeply scrutinize it. You're free from the experiences and notice who's left. You're in there and you know it. You exist regardless of the thoughts.

Consciousness is total awareness. There's nothing deeper or higher than it. If it didn't exist, there will be no you. Go deeper and dwell in the place of consciousness. It's where a genuine spiritual being exist, without power and intent. When you sit far back and look outside, you'll see every thought and emotion that passes before you. You're behind every single thing you see, just watching.

Chapter 4. The Lucid Self

The lucid dream is a kind of dream where you're aware that you're in a dream. You're sensible enough to realize what you're doing, like flying. This particular distinction is precisely the difference between being aware that you're conscious in your everyday life, and not knowing that you're aware. You're no longer entirely absorbed in the circumstances surrounding you when you're aware. You just continue to be aware on the inside, experiencing the events, as well as the thoughts and feelings. You're thinking of the thought and you know it. You're lucid.

Consciousness gives you the ability to focus. Awareness is the core of consciousness and it can direct itself on specific objects. It's a natural and intuitive aspect.

With your direct experience, you can learn more about consciousness. For instance, you realize that your consciousness can be aware of numerous objects, or it can be focused on just a single object, making you forget everything else.

If you step back, you'll see that objects are always passing before you in three different levels: physical, mental, and emotional. When you're not centered, your consciousness gets attracted toward one or more of those objects and focuses on them. If it concentrates enough, your sense of awareness loses itself in the object. It's like when you're watching television, you get absorbed in the screens of mind, emotions, and outside images. All of your senses are drawn in. If you wish to re-center, just start saying "hello" inside. Relax and be aware that you can hear it being echoed in your mind.

Imagine going to a movie theater. You can see, hear, taste, smell, and touch what you're viewing. When you begin to feel the character's emotions and think their thoughts, you now have a full dimension of the experience. However, when you become bored, you start thinking about other things. Your thoughts can still occur independently of the movie. They provide an alternative place for the consciousness to focus.

When you're not being aware that you're the one watching all this, you're lost. The lost soul is the consciousness that has dropped into the place where one human's thoughts, emotions, and sensory perceptions are all synchronized. The consciousness makes the mistake of focusing on one spot too closely. When the consciousness gets sucked in, it no longer knows itself as itself. It knows itself as the objects it is experiencing. You see yourself as these objects. Your entire existing self-concept is gone and replaced by the character on screen.

When the consciousness focuses on itself, you're contemplating the sources of consciousness. This is true meditation. It is beyond the act of simple, one-pointed concentration. The focus of consciousness is turned back to the Self. You achieve a completely different state. You're now aware of who you are. That is spirituality.

PART II:

Experiencing Energy

Chapter 5. Infinite Energy

Inner energy is one of life's mysteries. We always disregard the energy within. We think, feel, and act, but we don't understand what makes it possible for all these things to happen. The truth is, every body movement, emotion, and thought that passes through your mind is a use of energy. It's not only the events that happen in the physical world that require energy, but also everything that happens inside.

For instance, if you're thinking a specific thought and another thought steps in, you'll be forced to fight that impeding thought, which requires energy. If you're feeling an emotion that you don't like, you push it aside so it won't be able to disturb you. These acts use energy.

Creating thoughts, recalling thoughts, controlling emotions, producing emotions, and directing strong inner motivation all need a massive use of energy. You can feel the inner energy when you're excited or in love, but you can also feel emotionally and mentally drained sometimes. The source of energy is drawn from inside. It's different from the outside energy source.

Your energy level can hugely shift in an instant. One moment you can feel completely tired and drained and when something excites you, you jump like you're so full of energy. This is because you have an exceptional amount of inner energy. It's something that is always accessible to you. It replenishes, recharges, and restores you.

When you don't feel this energy inside of you, it's because you're blocking it by closing your heart and mind. You hide in a dark space. This is why you feel weak when you're sad or depressed. The heart, being a center of energy, can open or close. When it's closed, energy can't flow in.

It is the spiritual energy that you're experiencing when there's love in your heart. This energy is your inheritance and it's limitless. It's doesn't get tired and old. It simply needs willingness and openness. Everybody equally has this energy.

If you want to enjoy a full life and always experience high energy, enthusiasm and love, the first thing you need to do is to decide that you want to stay open. Closing your heart is a habit you can break and control.

You tend to open or close based on your past experiences. If it's something good, you open up. If it's a negative experience, you tend to close. It happens regularly throughout our daily lives.

The more you're open, the more energy can flow inside you. Don't let anything in life be too important that you're willing to close your heart. If you close your heart, you'll only end up locking yourself inside. Don't limit yourself. Life is meant to be fun, so let go and enjoy it.

Chapter 6. The Secrets of the Spiritual Heart

The heart is a masterpiece of creation. It's a wonderful instrument made of tremendously subtle energy. When you hear or feel an instrument, such as a piano or flute, you feel it because it has touched your heart.

Not all people understand the work of the heart. It experiences certain changes. When it's open, there's love. When it closes, the love ends. When it gets hurt, we feel empty. These shifts and variations of energy that occur in the heart run your life. Nevertheless, you are not your heart. You're the *experiencer* of the heart.

The heart is really easy to understand. It is a chakra, or a center of energy that influences our day-to-day lives. It controls the flow of energy by opening and closing. If you watch it, you know what it feels like when it's open or close. The state of your heart changes all the time. You can love someone and a few days later, you no longer feel anything.

As events happen, they come in through your physical senses and affects your inner state of being. These events can bring in fear, anxiety, or love. However, it's really energy that's coming inside you when you absorb the world. When energy patterns create a disruption in your psyche, then they get blocked because you don't let them pass through you. They are kept inside and they become a problem.

Perception allows you to experience what you take in. These experiences are how you learn and grow. Your mind and heart keep on expanding as you go through one moment to the next.

It's hard to keep energy together in one place for long. This is where the mind starts to become active. When the energy can't pass through the mind, it attempts to release through the heart, creating emotional activity. When you try to fight against that release, the energy gets stored deep within the heart. In fact, everything in your life that you didn't allow to pass through you is still inside you.

When very little energy comes into your mind and heart, everything can become dark and appear negative. Over time, your heart can still get blocked, but it can also open and close often, depending on your life experiences.

It's important to understand that most of what you take in passes through you. The only ones that get blocked are those that cause problems or some feeling of excitement. Thus, you can try to push energies away because they disturb you, or you try to keep energies because you like them. Either way, you're not allowing them to pass. You're wasting energy by blocking the flow by means of resisting or clinging.

Just enjoy the gift of life. This way, you'll certainly be pushed to the depth of your being. The energy flowing in your heart will raise and inspire you. Love will feed you and strengthen you. It's the strength that will carry you through life.

Chapter 7. Transcending the Tendency to Close

Everything that's happening inside has its foundation in a hidden energy field. The movements produce our emotional and mental patterns, including our automatic reaction, inner drive and urges. This internal force field is a hidden energy flowing in specific patterns into and out of your inner being.

It's easy to see that the central energy flow is the survival instinct. There's always been the daily struggle to protect and defend oneself, but this instinct underwent evolutionary changes. The protective energies adjusted toward protecting the person mentally, instead of physically. Nowadays, we defend our self-concepts instead of our bodies. We struggle not with the outside forces, but with our own internal fears and insecurities.

Since you can't run away, you just end up hiding inside and closing down. Even when you're not aware of your energy centers, you know how to close your heart even when you're still a kid. You protect the weak part of you even though there aren't any physical danger, but because you experience emotional problems.

You'll soon realize that if you keep on protecting yourself, you'll never be free. You're locking a scared person inside your heart. You'll never grow. You allow yourself to live with very little joy and you view life as a threat.

True spiritual growth takes place when every part of you is united. Pure energy flows inside of you and your consciousness is aware of it. To achieve this state, every piece of your self should be equally open to your awareness and released.

Inner energies are strong and powerful. Your consciousness can easily concentrate on disruption. They can pull your awareness into them, but you can stop and let go. You don't have to let yourself be dragged in there. This is why it's important to be centered. Otherwise, your consciousness will follow anything that grabs its attention.

Objects come and go, while your consciousness simply watches. Your consciousness remains constant. It experiences the formation of thoughts and emotions, and it can clearly see where they are coming from without thinking about it. Your psyche is simply watching the internal energies change based on the outside and inside forces.

A simple passing thought or emotion can eventually become the center of your life. If you don't let go, it can totally get out of control. Learn to relax and release. Be conscious enough to watch the part of you that's always trying to protect itself. Be determined to get rid of it. It will be the ultimate gift you can give yourself. You'll be free to walk in this world without having any problems. You get to enjoy and live in the present moment.

No one else can give or take your inner freedom from you, except yourself. Don't let yourself be bothered by little and meaningless things in life. Once you've learned to let go, you'll obtain peace even when you go through pain. You don't need to constantly pull yourself down. Make a decision to free yourself.

Part III:

Freeing Yourself

Chapter 8. Let Go Now or Fall

Self-exploration comes with life progression. Life has its ups and downs that can produce personal growth or personal fears. Whichever dominates depends on how we perceive change, which is something that's inevitable. It can either be frightening or exciting. Still, we must accept the fact that it is the nature of life.

What people don't realize is that fear is just another object that you can experience. You can choose to let go of it, or you can keep it and hide from it. Some people try to create a safe place for themselves so they define how they need life to be, which really makes the world frightening. When you're afraid, life throws in circumstances that challenge your attempts to be safe. You struggle with life because you resist change.

It's the fear inside us that tells us that we should determine how life should be. It prevents us from facing reality because it's beyond our control. Don't define the outside world based on your inner problems. It will surely be a terrible mess.

Protecting yourself from problems will only generate more problems. Dialogues keep going inside your head because you're trying to figure out how to stop or deal with the events that are happening. Choose not to go against life. You'll never get to fully live it if you keep on controlling it because life is constantly changing. It's possible to live without fear.

Life comes up with circumstances that push you out of your comfort zone, trying to remove what's blocking you inside. Fear is actually caused by the blockages in the energy flow. The energy can't feed your heart and your heart becomes weak, making it prone to fear.

If you want spiritual growth, you must understand that keeping things inside will only keep you trapped. After some time, you'll be wanting to free yourself. You'll realize that there are many things surrounding you that promote growth. You see it as a great opportunity to let go.

When you suddenly get pulled down into the disturbed energy, everything looks dark and depressing because you're watching from the seat of disturbance. This should remind you to let go. Otherwise, you'll only try hard to fix things. You can't clearly see what's happening. You just want the agitation to stop. Hence, you turn to your survival instincts because you want to get away from the things you don't like.

This leads to you falling into the darkness and manifesting it. You put negative energy into your environment and it comes back to you. This is precisely how people destroy relationships, as well as their lives.

All you have to do is to let go right from the start to avoid all these mess. Open up and release the blocked energy. Let it flow up until it fuses back into your own consciousness. This will strengthen you. Always look up and get up. It is the secret of ascension. It's the secret of rising from below.

Chapter 9. Removing Your Inner Thorn

The spiritual journey is an endless transformation. You can't stay the same if you want to grow. Always embrace change. The way we find solutions to our own problems requires change. Once you accept your problems and see them as an opportunity for growth, that's the beginning of real transformation.

Imagine there's a thorn in your arm. When it is touched, you feel the pain. You only have two choices. You can either see to it that nothing touches the thorn or you can remove it from your arm. Your choices will set the course of your entire life.

If you choose the first option, you'll be working all your life to protect the thorn. Your whole life revolves around it and you might even be proud of it. You may think you have come up with a solution to your problem, but you really don't. You let this thorn run your life. It affects every decision you make every single day.

When you protect yourself from your problems, it only reflects the problem itself. You didn't solve the main cause of it; you just dedicated your whole life to staying away from it.

Notice that whenever you have a problem, instead of asking yourself how to get rid of it, you ask how you can protect yourself from feeling it. Even if you avoid situations that would make you feel or think about the problem, it will always keep on coming back. Your core problem will only expand into several problems. It affects everything around you, including your behavior.

When it comes to the human heart, we have plenty of thorns. When something touches them, it causes pain inside. Just like a person living with a thorn stuck in his arm, you end up restricting yourself. You need to make a choice. You can always choose to take out your inner thorns. It's the only way you can be totally free of them. Most importantly, don't question your capacity to get rid of the main source of the distress inside you.

In order to free yourself, you must find yourself. You're not the pain and you're not the part, which always stresses out. They have nothing to do with you. You're the one who notices these things. You can let them come up, but you can also let them go. Your inner thorns are just blocked energies from the past, which can be released. There's no reason to keep them.

Energies have been inside you your entire life. If you become aware, you'll notice that they're not you. You're simply experiencing and feeling them. If you remain centered, you'll learn to respect and appreciate your experiences, even when they seem to be difficult. When you're in the seat of consciousness, you'll experience your inner being's spirit and strength even when your heart feels weak. This is the core of the path to a spiritual life.

Chapter 10. Stealing Freedom for Your Soul

To attain true freedom, you must decide not to suffer anymore. There is no need to carry the burden brought by pain, fear, or sorrow. People only suffer because they don't know what it's like to not suffer.

What really goes on with the emotional and mental energies inside of you is that your inner vulnerability constantly brings you to a situation in which you're suffering. You're either striving to avoid or make the suffering stop, or worry about it in the next days to come.

When your suffering gets worse, that's the time you notice it and admit that you have a problem. It creates an impact on your behavior and your inner voice gets anxious. You always think about yourself because you're not okay inside. You're always trying to make yourself feel better. You go around trying to change things around you so you can please yourself. You must understand and accept that your psyche is not okay, but it can be all right. When fear is present, that's your psyche trying to talk to you.

Your psyche becomes afraid when you mistreat it. You're providing it with certain responsibilities that are impossible to understand. For instance, you keep on thinking about trying to please everyone all the time. The mind has to make sure everything goes your way. You're giving it an impossible task. It's like forcing your body to lift huge trees.

When you worry about yourself, you suffer. Your thoughts are directed towards what's troubling you at the moment. Your mind tells you that there's something outside that needs to change to solve your inner problems. However, it's not a good advice. Because your mind is disturbed by fears, it can misguide you.

Outside situations only try to solve the problem, not to cause inner problems. For instance, if you feel lonely, being in a relationship is your effort to solve your problem. You're trying to find out if that relationship will calm your internal disturbance. Still, it's not the solution to the source of your problem.

On the other hand, to achieve success in terms of your psyche, you shouldn't think about it or dedicate your life to it. Imagine what it's like without those upsetting thoughts. You can truly live and experience life, instead of trying to fix yourself.

You can live a life without the fear of your "self". All you have to do is to stop forcing the mind to fix your own problems. It cannot manipulate everything around you. If it's trying to talk to you, ignore it. Once you're okay with everything, then everything will be okay.

Relax and be quiet. You're not the thinking mind. You're simply aware of it. You're the consciousness behind it that's aware of the thoughts. You watch the mind think. This way, you're actually liberating yourself.

Chapter 11. Pain, the Price of Freedom

Change isn't always comfortable. It challenges what we know and questions our needs. It is often recognized as a heartbreaking experience. Coming to peace with pain is necessary for personal transformation and spiritual growth. You must be able to face your inner disturbances. You'll then realize that pain is seated in the core of your heart, which is why you spend your life trying to avoid it.

Pain can influence everything you do. Unlike physical pain, inner pain always exists. It only hides underneath your thoughts and emotions. You can really feel it when your heart goes into confusion. If you really want to grow, you must learn to deal with pain.

Any behavior pattern based on the prevention of pain turns into a doorway to pain itself. The feelings you experience will work their way back to the motive behind your actions. For instance, if you're scared of being rejected and you approach a person, when that person says something wrong, you'll feel the pain of rejection.

Pain comes from the heart. This is the reason why you feel a lot of agitation throughout the day. The pain that is not processed creates more layers of sensitivities every time you try to avoid it. For example, in order to keep your friendship with others, everything you do must be acceptable to them. You think about several ways to present yourself. You've gone layers and layers and further away from the core pain. You end up becoming so sensitive that everything you do affects your heart and causes pain.

You need to get some perspective to distance yourself from this. Walk outside or stare at the night sky. There are billions of stars in the galaxy and you're just standing on a ball of dirt, spinning around one of those stars. From that point of view, would you really care what other people think of you?

You can choose to leave the pain inside and keep struggling with the outside, or you can get rid of the inner pain. You can only be free if you don't let pain run your life. Think of the inner pain as a temporary shift in the flow of your energy. You don't have to be afraid of the experience. You can't spend your life avoiding things that are not even happening. Pain can just be a feeling that you can handle. Whatever happens, you're okay with it. It can't touch you unless you touch it.

Don't let pain shape you, your thoughts, reactions, and preferences. You must learn to go beyond your habit of avoiding pain. Many things happen every day that cause an inner disturbance. Stop fighting your feelings. Pain is simply an energy that you must allow to pass through.

There are freedom and joy on the other side of pain. You must be willing to accept pain to pass through to the other side. Once you feel comfortable with it, there's no reason to be scared of yourself. There's nothing that the world can do to hurt you. You're free. Pain is the price of freedom.

Part IV:

Going Beyond

Chapter 12. Taking Down the Walls

As you continue to grow, your inner "self" becomes a lot quieter. You'll realize that you've been in there this whole time. It's just that you've been overwhelmed by this flood of thoughts and emotions. You'll start to think that it's actually possible to surpass all these disruptions. Since you're completely separated from the things you're watching, there's a way to be free from the hold that your psyche has over your awareness.

Enlightenment is the inner breakthrough to complete freedom. However, the term itself is often misunderstood since it is based on our limited understanding and personal experiences.

Take this story as an example. Imagine you're in a beautiful open place with great light. You immediately decided that you wanted to live there. You bought it and started to build your dream house. It even has separate quarters so your housekeeper could leave you alone. When it was finished, you loved every part of it because you put your heart and soul into every aspect of the house.

Over time, you started spending more time indoors until you

became used to living safely within the confines of the house. Inside the house, everything was predictable, familiar, and within your control. Meanwhile, the outside world was uncertain, unknown, and out of your control.

You got so used to never turn off the lights, but eventually they started burning so you had to use a few candles. It was hard for you because you're a person who loves light. Still, your fears about leaving the safety of your house are much stronger. The darkness eventually harmed your physical and mental health. What was once a beautiful place started to fade from your mind.

Soon, you became lonely. You forgot why you're so scared. You're just aware of being so uncomfortable. You even stopped doing the things you love. You were falling into the darkness.

All of a sudden, your housekeeper called you down to the storage cellar. You were surprised to see it fully radiant because of all these emergency flashlights stored in there. It became a turning point in your life.

You began creating beauty, light, and happiness within your house. You worked together to keep the light shining brightly. Love began to shine in both of your hearts. You even married each other and promised to bring light and love into your home. It was heaven.

One day, you came across a book in your library that talked about the natural light that exists outside. You felt so confused because you've been living for so long inside that dark house that you don't know how to go outside.

That house is all your thoughts, emotions, past experiences, and dreams. You pulled and knit them all together into a conceptual world in which you live. This mental structure blocks you from whatever natural light is on the outside.

Don't be afraid to go past these walls. Don't hide in the darkness. You can get out by letting life take down your walls. When your walls crumble down and consciousness is released, flourishing in its own brilliance, that is true enlightenment.

Chapter 13. Far, Far Beyond

Going beyond simply means going past where you are. You don't just stay in your present situation. There are no boundaries or limitations when you always go beyond yourself. Beyond is immeasurable in all ways. The truth is, everything is limitless. Things only appear to be limited because your consciousness runs into mental boundaries.

You must keep going past the limits you put on things so you can go beyond. This means changing something within yourself. Right now, your logical mind creates an alternative reality of limited thoughts that remain fixed in your head. This is because you want to try to control things. You end up constantly struggling to fit certain pieces together to make a world that fits your model of reality. If things don't fit, you label them as bad or wrong.

When something happens that challenges your perception of things, you get frustrated and you fight. If you wish to surpass it, you must not believe in it. Try understanding why you built a mental model in the first place and see what happens when it doesn't work. You actually end up struggling to keep your world from collapsing.

Your world doesn't need to fall apart for you to realize what you're doing. If you want to see why you do certain things, don't do them. For instance, if you want to know the reason you're smoking, then stop smoking. See what happens when you don't do the things that make you comfortable. You always try to stay within your comfort zone. Otherwise, you feel uncomfortable and your mind tells you to fix things. Everything you do keeps you restricted.

You can choose to remain in your comfort zone or you can work on your freedom. Imagine what it's like to be like a tiger inside a cage. It can be extremely frightening. Your comfort zone creates a similar cage. It doesn't limit your body; it limits the area of your consciousness.

Fear makes you want to stay inside this cage. You're afraid because what's beyond is unknown to you. You want to feel safe that's why you don't want to get out. You have fallen in love with your cage.

When you are spiritually awake, you'll realize that you are locked up in a cage. You're always hitting the walls of your comfort zone. You start to see that you can't freely express yourself because you're too self-conscious. Since you've set some limits on yourself, once you approach your limits, you start to feel anxious and insecure.

The moment you're willing to go beyond and face reality without mental boundaries, your soul becomes free and infinite. You go on your day with an inspired and peaceful heart. Spirituality is the commitment to go beyond, no matter what it takes.

Chapter 14. Letting Go of False Solidity

The psyche is a complex place with conflicting forces that keeps on changing due to external and internal events. In just a short amount of time, various fears, needs, and desires build up and we end up struggling to hold it all together. We spend most of our time trying to control and keep everything in order.

When you struggle, you suffer. Trying to hold everything together is already a form of suffering, especially when things start to fall apart. Your psyche becomes troubled and you fight to keep your innermost world together. Nevertheless, the truth is, there's nothing solid in there in which you can cling to.

As you go deeper into yourself, you'll realize that your consciousness is always there. It's a dynamic field of awareness that can broadly expand or narrowly focus. Your sense of self is then determined by where you are directing your consciousness.

When you become focused on a particular object, it moves slowly. The force of consciousness ends up holding the objects steady just by focusing on it. This act creates clinging.

When you cling to a specific thought or emotions, it can remain in one place long enough to block the psyche.

The objects you cling to are used to create a sense of orientation and security in the middle of the nonstop inner change. You make a structure of clear solidity and you end up building your entire self around it. However, you'll never find yourself in what you have built to define yourself. You just allowed yourself to become lost.

Your sense of stability creates a false sense of security. As a result, when you can't anticipate the behavior of the people around you, it disturbs you.

People put facades out there. All of us are always clinging and building. We try to create someone and when that someone is what others want and need, you can be quite popular and successful. The society has a lot to say about everything. Think about it. When people behave based on your expectations, you treat them nicely, but when they don't, you either pull back from them or get angry.

What people don't know is that the clinging can stop. You don't have to hold on to your experiences in order to build yourself. You just need to be brave enough to let go and face your fears. Let the moments come and go. It's the only way you can stop struggling and attain peace. When you don't take part in this struggle, you can live spiritually.

You don't have to live like everybody else. You can be completely free to experience life. You can be filled with light and your inner force will guide you from the inside. You'll be at peace. When you're at peace with your true being, there's no room for false solidity.

Part V:

Living Life

Chapter 15. The Path of Unconditional Happiness

Life itself is the highest path to spirituality. Everything becomes a liberating experience when you know how to live your everyday life. To do this, you only have to make one choice. You need to decide if you want to be happy or not. If you choose to be happy, then your life path becomes absolutely clear.

People usually don't give themselves a choice because they think it's beyond their control. Their number of preferences gets in the way. If you really want to be happy, say it without any limitations to it. You must want it regardless of what happens in life. There shouldn't be any ands, buts, or ifs. You'll only give a limit to your happiness if you create a condition. Your choice must be unconditional. You must really mean it when you say that you want to be happy. Unconditional happiness is the biggest means there is. You'll not only be happy, but you'll also be enlightened.

The moment you decide to be happy, challenges will become inevitable. Your commitment will be put to the test, which ultimately promotes spiritual growth. It's really not easy to be happy when everything isn't going well.

The purpose of life is to enjoy and learn from your experiences. You're not born to suffer. Being miserable doesn't help anybody. You came into this world and you're going to die. What you do during your time in between is your choice. It's not the events that determine whether you're going to be happy or not. You get to choose that for yourself.

Let go of the part of you that constantly creates melodrama. The only sensible thing to do is to enjoy life's experiences. There's nothing you can gain out of pain and suffering, so don't let the things you can't control bother you.

Choosing to enjoy life is a spiritual teacher itself. Once you commit to unconditional happiness, you'll learn more about yourself, about others, and about life. You'll learn more about your heart and mind. Always stay open. It also helps to use affirmations. If you commit yourself to being happy, nothing would be able to stop you.

The key is to understand your inner energies. If you look deep within yourself, you'll find that your heart feels open when you're happy and energy keeps flowing inside. Don't try to close your heart whenever you feel sad. You have that choice to not give up your happiness.

If you stay open, positive energy will surely fill your heart. Spiritual practices bear fruit when you learn to stay open. You'll never know how many great things you can find. It's possible to reach the state of bliss and freedom. The joy you feel can become overpowering, and it's such a beautiful path to take.

Chapter 16. The Spiritual Path of Nonresistance

Your spiritual work must lead towards learning to live a life without fears, problems, stress, or melodrama. Stress only happens when you resist the changes in life's events. When you simply live in the present, you won't create any resistance. You're just witnessing and experiencing life as it happens.

You must first understand why you try so hard to defy life. If you look within yourself, you'll find that it's actually you who has this certain kind of power. It's called willpower.

Will is a force that springs from your being. It's what makes your body move. You use the same will to hold on to your thoughts when you want to focus on them. It's also what you use when you try to make things happen, or when you prevent something from happening. You have the power to influence things.

Trying to resist the things that happened doesn't change the fact that they still happened. What you're really trying to resist is the experience passing through you and it will only affect you inside.

In time, you'll realize that this resistance is just a waste of energy. You're basically using your willpower to resist the outcomes from the past or thoughts about the future. Anything you do will just cause more disturbance. The energy that needs to be released has no place to go. It gets stuck in your psyche and severely affects you.

Because we tend to struggle with past energies, we become unprepared to face the present events. Over time, we become so blocked that we get stressed-out or completely burned-out.

The personal events that happen in our lives leave marks on our hearts and minds. They become the foundation for our will to either cling or resist. Because of these, you resist the current events, which creates inner struggle and tension. You think these past events have meaning, but the truth is, they just ruin your life.

You need to use life and be very conscious. You need to cautiously watch the mental voice as it tries to speak to you. It will give you advice and tell you to resist the world, but don't listen to it. Let your spiritual path become the willingness to allow whatever happens pass through you. Start by dealing with every situation with acceptance. Accept that events are not personal problems, they're just events taking place in this world.

Take a pause and think about what you're capable of achieving if you don't let your inner struggles restrain you. The world eventually becomes a different place. You could actually do anything. You could transform your life if you let your heart and mind become open and wide enough to embrace reality. You'll feel more love, peace, and contentment.

Chapter 17. Contemplating Death

It is indeed a great contradiction that death turns out to be one of life's best teachers. Death teaches you things that nothing else and no else can teach you. However, the real question is, are you going to wait that long and let death become your teacher?

A wise individual understands that at any time or place, his life can be taken away from him. He embraces the fact that death is unpredictable and inevitable.

Death doesn't have to be the one things that challenge you to live at your highest level. You don't have to wait until everything is gone before you learn to dig down deep within yourself to reach your highest potential. The moment you realize this, it's actually the consciousness you need to create deep and meaningful relationships.

People usually take things for granted because they think that other people would still be there when they wake up the next day. But what if they aren't? Imagine what it would be like to live like every person you care about could be taken away at any moment. Your life will surely be different.

Death is not a morbid thought. In fact, it's a wonderful idea that you can think about. Surely, if you know that you could be taking your last breath at any moment, then you wouldn't waste your time and energy focusing on things that don't really matter. With this truth in mind, you should be brave enough to constantly reflect on how you're living your life. People who have experienced true awakening fully live their lives without making any compromises.

You don't have to be afraid to talk about death. Instead, allow this knowledge to help you or guide you on how to live every moment of your life, because every single one of them matters. Everything can be a million times more meaningful.

Death can change everything in an instant. When you embrace this truth, you don't really have to change your life, just the way you live it. It's not about what you're doing, it's how much of you is doing it.

Start using every day to say what you need to say and do what you need to do. Be fully present without fearing what could happen next. Don't fear death. Instead, allow it to free you. Allow it to encourage you to live your life to the fullest. Live as if you're facing death all the time. Don't be afraid of life. Growth from experience is the only thing you can get from it. The willingness to live is what gives life meaning. Death makes life precious.

Chapter 18. The Secret of the Middle Way

The path to spiritual life isn't complete without addressing one of the deepest of all spiritual teachings, the *Tao te Ching*. "The Tao" means "the Way." It is so delicate that people only talk around its edges, but never truly touch it. It is a treatise in which the very basis for the principles of all of life is laid down.

Unfortunately, many spiritual teachings hide the center of truth with mystical words. Nevertheless, with Tao, it's simple. People who have truly learned the secrets of life understand these truths without reading anything. If you want to understand Tao, you must take it slow and keep it simple. Otherwise, you may miss it even when it's already right in front of you.

Everything has two extremes and the Tao is in the middle. It's the place where there is the balance. There's no energy pushing it in either direction. Everything remains in peaceful harmony.

You have to realize that everything has its yin and yang and its own balance point. It's the order of all these balance points, woven together, that forms the Tao. This overall balance maintains its equilibrium as it moves through time and space. Energies are pulled to the center so that it wouldn't be wasted going sideways. Staying centered gets something done.

In every aspect of life, if you're in balance, your body stays healthy. Being in extremes also teaches you many things. When you analyze them, it's easy to see the results of imbalanced behavior patterns.

The more extreme you are, the less forward movement there is. You only end up getting stuck. Simply let the extremes go. You'll see that all the energy that had been wasted will be easily accessible to you. You'll become much clearer and the experience of being present in each moment will become a natural state for you. Events that take place in life will no longer appear confusing or overwhelming.

Almost everyone has a point at which they get out of balance. However, whoever stays present with the fixture of purpose always ends up coming out on top.

When you move in the Tao, life becomes totally simple. Life unfolds while you feel for the center. All things move quietly through that center balance. The Tao is there in everything. It is completely at peace. You can't touch it, but you can be at one with it.

Chapter 19. The Loving Eyes of God

We all have different teachings, concepts, and views about God, but how can anyone really know anything about Him? Fortunately, there's a direct connection to the Divine deep within us. There's a part of our being that's beyond the personal self and you can consciously choose to identify with that part. It's where a natural transformation starts to take place inside of you. You can know the nature of God by looking into the mirror of your changed "self". This is a direct experience.

Over time, you'll start to stray away from the feelings of tension and anxiety. Although the cloud of lower vibrations may still be there, you stop thinking they're you or that there's anything you have to do about them. Your Spirit drifts upward as you learn to let go of them. You know it because you experience it.

Your being draws further back inside yourself. You start to feel more spaciousness inside. You don't feel fear, anger, or resentment towards other people. You don't close your heart. You feel like you're going somewhere and you're actually going into your spiritual being. You identify more with the flow of pure energy.

Now you walk around feeling love for no reason. The Spirit always feels good, open and light. Because of this, you center more and more on the spiritual part of your being. As you willingly release the physical, mental and emotional aspects of your being, the Spirit becomes your state. Everything becomes more beautiful.

Still, how can you really know God or anything that's beyond you? You know because the people who have gone beyond came back and told you that the Spirit you're experiencing is the gateway to God. They have felt great love and light waking up inside them and their sense of Self-merging with it. Just like what's stated in the Gospel of John, that one can merge into God. This is how you know Him. You become one with Him.

Imagine what would happen if you begin to feel great love towards every creature. There's no judgment. There's only loving, respecting and appreciating.

Knowing God must come from actual experience. It's what happens when you meditate, or let go of your lower "self". You drift into Spirit and transformations happen inside of you. You just need to notice them. You'll get a glimpse of what it must be like to sit in that Divine State.

There's no impurity. Everything is just beautiful. You

embrace other people's whole being. That's how it is through the eyes of love. If God is love, the eyes are filled with endless love and compassion. And indeed, you have a loving God.

Conclusion

Life can be really simple. All you have to do is just to know your inner "self". There's truly more to everything than we thought we already know. It's such a great way to live knowing that there's more to learn when you've uncovered one of life's greatest mysteries.

No matter what you say or do, or where you go, there is always you. You are always conscious of the things passing through your physical senses. It's just that sometimes, you get too distracted with the opposing voices going on inside your head. You don't have to listen to those voices. You just need to let it go.

Your life depends on you, not on the things around you. The outside world is full of chaos that once you let it affect you, you can easily fall into the trap of darkness. Keep your heart open and don't lock yourself inside whenever things don't go your way. The ability to live freely is within you. Positive energies are always available inside of you, if only you'll learn how to release the negative thoughts and emotions that's usually dragging you down.

If you want to grow, don't let fear take control over you. It only leads to more pain and suffering. If you surrender to fear, you'll end up locking yourself in a cage. You're depriving yourself of the great things that the world can still offer you. Take the steps toward the other side of fear. There you'll find freedom, joy, and love.

Learn to accept that life will continue to unfold no matter what you do and the events won't always be what you expect them to be. You can't control everything, but don't let it stop you from being happy. Instead, when bad things happen, you simply experience it and learn from it. You don't have to cling to it. Let it all go and keep moving forward.

Life isn't about trying to please everyone. Your happiness doesn't depend on anyone. The outside world won't be able to solve the real problem that's inside of you. Be conscious enough not to torture your mind thinking about how you should live your life to be accepted by others. You can stop listening to your thoughts and let all the melodrama simply slip through your mind. Be who you really are.

While pain can be uncomfortable, you can see it as a way to grow spiritually. Go beyond your comfort zone. Experience life. It's all about making a choice between being happy and being miserable. Surely, you don't want to pick the latter. Nothing is worth being miserable over.

Don't waste your precious time and energy doing things that

stop you from freely expressing yourself. You don't need to hide in the dark. Follow your heart and experience life. It is God's greatest gift to you because God is love. Walk towards the path of light and happiness. Live with absolute freedom and love. You can always choose to live a meaningful and beautiful life.

FREE BONUSES

P.S. Is it okay if we overdeliver?

Here at Readtrepreneur Publishing, we believe in overdelivering way beyond our reader's expectations. Is it okay if we overdeliver?

Here's the deal, we're going to give you an extremely condensed PDF summary of the book which you've just read and much more…

What's the catch? We need to trust you… You see, we want to overdeliver and in order for us to do that, we've to trust our reader to keep this bonus a secret to themselves? Why? Because we don't want people to be getting our exclusive PDF summaries even without buying our books itself. Unethical, right?

Ok. Are you ready?

Firstly, remember that your book is code: **"READ120"**.

Next, visit this link: **http://bit.ly/exclusivepdfs**

Everything else will be self explanatory after you've visited: **http://bit.ly/exclusivepdfs**.

We hope you'll enjoy our free bonuses as much as we enjoyed preparing it for you!

CPSIA information can be obtained
at www.ICGtesting.com
Printed in the USA
BVHW080931030919
557435BV00001B/53/P

9 781690 401537